Speckly Weckly Freckly Dots

Written and Illustrated by Sara Lewis

Southern Lion Books

First Printing

Published by
Southern Lion Books
Children's Publications
1280 Westminster Way
Madison, Georgia 30650

southernlionbooks.com

Manufactured in the United States of America.

Library of Congress Control Number 2009943260

ISBN 978-1-935272-05-2

The paper in this book meets the guidelines for permanence and durability
of the Committee on Production Guidelines for Book Longevity of the
Council on Library Resources.

This book is dedicated
to my husband David

~because you knew I could

Special thanks to my mother Ruth Sarrett

~couldn't have done it without you

Mr. Freckles was a horse
who lived on a farm.
He played in a pasture
and slept in a barn.
As you can tell
by Mr. Freckles' name,
he had several freckles
below his mane.

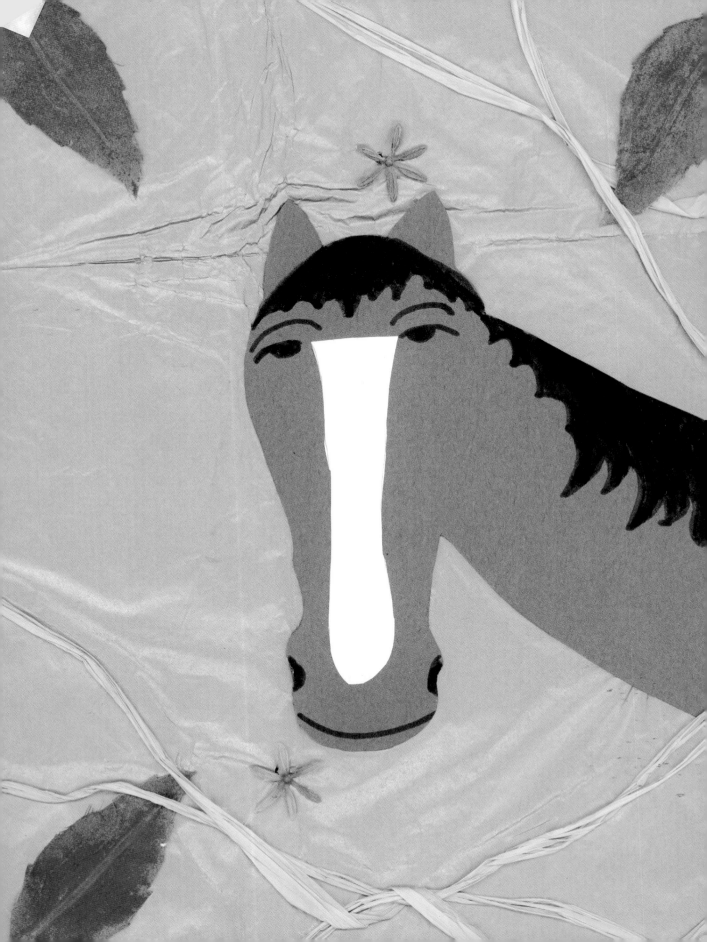

Mr. Freckles did not care
for his speckled face.
He wanted his
freckles to disappear
POOF! Without a trace.

He said to himself,

"Speckly weckly freckly dots,
I do not like these tiny spots!"

Mr. Freckles imagined that he could change.
He wanted to be new,
even silly or strange.

He thought to himself,
"I wish I had wings
to soar through the air,
fly above the clouds
without a care.

But nope, I just have speckly weckly freckly dots,
I do not like these tiny spots!"

"I wish I had fins
to swim through the sea,
a life under water
would be perfect for me!

But nope, I just have speckly weckly freckly dots,
I do not like these tiny spots!"

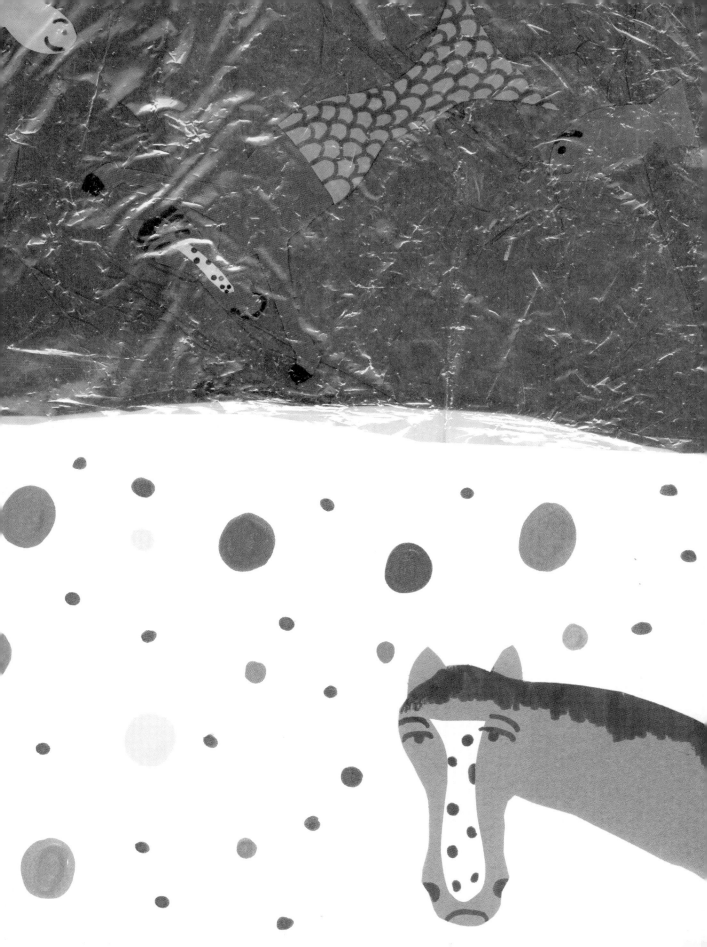

"I wish I could slither
like a snake on my tummy,
twisting and turning
and curling so funny!

Sigh-
But nope, I just have speckly weckly freckly dots,
I do not like these tiny spots!"

On a bright sunny day
a stranger came to the farm,
a sweet young girl
full of smiles and charm.

Mr. Freckles liked the new guest,
with her sweet voice and kind eyes.
She was there to choose a horse and much to
Mr. Freckles' surprise...

She took one look at him and smiled
from ear to ear.

"This is the one, Mommy!
This one right here!
He has freckles on his nose,
just like I wish I had!"

This surprised Mr. Freckles,
for his speckles made him mad.

He loved his new friend,
his freckles he did
not need to hide.
She loved Mr. Freckles' speckles,
and of course
the horse inside.

Mr. Freckles is now
happy and proud,
he sings a new song
and he sings it out loud.

Mr. Freckles and the author, Sara Lewis, on her wedding day

Photo courtesy of Jeff Miller